L O V E
D O E S
STUDY GUIDE

FIVE SESSIONS

LOVE

DISCOVER A SECRETLY INCREDIBLE LIFE
IN AN ORDINARY WORLD

DOES

STUDY GUIDE

BOB GOFF

WITH DIXON KINSER

THOMAS NELSON

Since 1798

NASHVILLE   DALLAS   MEXICO CITY   RIO DE JANEIRO

Published in Nashville, Tennessee, by Thomas Nelson. Thomas Nelson is a registered
trademark of Thomas Nelson, Inc.

Thomas Nelson, Inc., titles may be purchased in bulk for educational, business, fund-
raising, or sales promotional use. For information, please e-mail SpecialMarkets@
ThomasNelson.com.

ISBN-13: 978-1-4002-0627-8

Printed in the United States of America
14 15 16 17 QG 7 6 5 4 3 2

CONTENTS

INTRODUCTION

What do I do to live into the person that Jesus made me to be?...
Do you know what the answer was for me? I did stuff!

Loves Does *video*

Welcome to *Love Does*!

All of us have seasons of life when our relationship with God is really humming—those times where our faith and life sync up in all the right ways and everything just works. We also have the other kind of season. You know the one I mean: the season where faith and life seem to butt heads. Life gets hard, faith seems stale, and we feel stuck. If you've ever felt like that, then don't go anywhere—this study is for you!

You see, this is a study about God's love ... and the most amazing thing about that love is that it's not just a bunch of rules or stuff we have to agree with. God's love is different. It changes things. It brings hope where before there was only despair. It revives faith that feels lifeless. It makes a way forward where there seems to be only a dead end. It's active. It works. It risks. God's love ... *does.*

7

Tapping into this love requires a different skill set than what it takes to memorize answers for a test or to follow all the traffic laws so you don't get a ticket. This isn't a love you can earn, buy, or win. It's something better. Something bigger. And it just might be something you discover more about by "doing stuff" too.

That's what this study is all about.

Love Does is a five-week experiment in *doing* the love of God. Each session will explore a different aspect of God's active love through the teachings and stories of Bob Goff. There will be an opening question, a short Bible study, and then a video featuring Bob. However, the real action comes after the video when you dig into each topic in a guided small group time. Here's where the rubber meets the road and you see how God's love gets practical as you are invited to join in it too. It's going to be great. Really. However, if you want to get the most out of your *Love Does* experience, it's best to keep a few things in mind.

First, the real growth in this study will happen during your small group time. This is where you will process the content of Bob's message, ask questions, and learn from others as you listen to what God's love is doing in their lives. This leads to point two. Small groups can be a deeply rewarding time of intimacy and friendship, but they can also be a disaster. Work to make your group a safe place. That means being honest about your own thoughts and feelings as well as listening carefully to everyone else's. Third, resist the temptation to "fix" a problem someone might be having or to correct someone's theology. That's not what this time is for. Finally, keep everything your group shares confidential. All this will foster a rewarding sense of community in your *Love Does* group and give God's Spirit the space to heal, challenge, and send you out to *do* the love of God.

HOW TO USE THIS GUIDE

As you'll discover throughout this study, love is practical. It gets out there and does things. It takes risks. Bob found the most vitality in his faith when he was trying new things and "doing stuff." This study is designed to give you similar opportunities.

Each session in *Love Does* begins with a mixer question followed by a reflection from the Bible. Then you'll watch Bob's video teaching and jump into some directed small group discussion. There are multiple questions to choose from, so don't feel as if you have to use them all. Your leader will focus on the ones that resonate with your group and guide you from there.

The final component of each session is called "Putting Love into Action." Here *Love Does* might diverge from other studies you may have done, as you and your group will engage in one hands-on exercise that "does" the love of God the way Bob described in the video. These exercises are designed to be completed during your meeting and will be as valuable as what you make them. If you choose to only go through the motions (or abstain from participating), chances are you'll find them less than satisfying. But if you take the gamble, you may discover what so many others have already found to be true: faith comes alive when we take holy risks for God.

Now, we realize that the thought of "risky" activities can make some folks feel anxious. That's okay. If you fall into this category, just check out each "Putting Love into Action" exercise ahead of time. Then you can prepare yourself accordingly. And remember, none of these experiments involve anything weird or embarrassing. They are just opportunities to show love in tangible ways.

At the end of each session are further suggestions for you to engage the content of *Love Does* between group meetings. This section, entitled "What Love Does This Week," includes activities developed around action (called *Do*), Bible study (called *Reflect*), and a reading from the *Love Does* book (called *Read*). You are invited to do *at least* one of these activities between sessions and to use your study guide to record what you learned. Some weeks there will be more options than others. Your job is to pray and choose which will challenge you most as you put God's love into action. Starting in Session 2, time is given to revisit the on-your-own activities and process them as a group. And, if you could not do an activity one week or are just joining the study, don't worry. Hearing what others have learned will be nourishment enough.

Finally, remember that this *Love Does* study is meant to help train participants in a new way of thinking about love. The videos, discussions, and activities are all meant to kick-start your imagination so that you start coming up with new ideas and "doing stuff" on your own. Just imagine what God could do with a whole group of people who were passionate about Jesus' love and eager to put it into creative practice? Let's jump into *Love Does* and find out.

If you are a group leader, additional instructions and resources for leading the "What Love Does This Week" sections are found in the back of this guide. Because some of the activities require materials and setup, make sure you read these instructions ahead of time so that you are adequately prepared.

I'M WITH YOU

Love is not just a bunch of stuff we agree with. Love does.

Loves Does *video*

INTRODUCTION

Have you ever had to do something you were afraid to do? Sure. Everyone has. It is a core part of the human experience. Whether it is jumping off a high dive, riding a bike for the first time, or even professing love, everyone at some point has to do something he or she is scared of—and that's a good thing. Good because these experiences teach us important lessons about being human and about our life with God.

First, when we do things that we are afraid of we learn that courage is not the same thing as the absence of fear. The first time a child dives into a swimming pool, it is a terrifying experience and no amount of explaining, hand-holding, or encouragement will make the fear go away. To dive into the pool, the child will have to act *in spite of* her fear. That is the definition of courage. Acting, even when you are afraid, is something people who are called to follow Jesus have to do all the time.

Second, after we do something that frightens us the first time, the second time is never as hard. And it is even easier the third time. Though the first jump off the diving board may be terrifying, by the third or fourth time you do it, it may start to be downright fun.

All this brings us to the third thing we learn. You may be thinking, *I have a solution for this whole tension—I'll avoid risky situations at all costs.* The problem with this is (1) no one has that much control over life, and (2) these moments of risk are when we truly feel most alive. Have you ever seen a kid go over a skateboard ramp for the first time? Or watched someone complete a tall rock climb? Often you'll find them screaming in celebration. Why? Because they just feel so alive! Because they did it! When we try things that seem daunting, our lives actually become more full and vibrant.

So, how does God factor into all of this? And what does any of it have to do with *Love Does*? The *Love Does* experience will encourage you to get out there and "do" things! You will be invited, through the sharing and activities in each session, to engage in some holy risk taking. Please, take this invitation seriously and don't let the opportunity pass you by. Like riding a bike for the first time, the more activities and experiments you try, the less scary they become—because they turn into things you do all the time. Furthermore, every time you participate in the hands-on portions of this study you'll be training yourself to see the world as a place where you can act creatively for and with God. You'll become the kind of person who "does" love effortlessly, just as Jesus did.

For this first session of *Love Does*, Bob asks if you have ever felt stuck trying to integrate your life and your faith. Maybe there was a time when following Jesus was exciting and vibrant, but now things have started to grow stale. Do you know what he's talking about? One of the reasons our life with God gets stagnant is because we stop taking Jesus' invitation to live risky, courageous lives. We stop trying to do the things Jesus calls us to because they seem too scary. This week *Love Does* is going to provide a platform for you to be fully alive, to take risks, and get involved in bringing heaven to earth. Are you ready? Well, actually, that doesn't matter. Let's just jump in with both feet. And if you need to scream ... all the better!

WELCOME AND CHECKING IN

Go around the group to introduce yourselves and then complete this sentence:

If I could describe my expectations for this study in one word, that word would be _____.

Next, watch the short video clip titled "Introduction." Afterward, answer some or all of the following questions:

- On a scale of "thumbs-up" for positive and "thumbs-down" for negative, what was your gut reaction to Bob's introduction?
- When it comes to integrating your faith and your life, have you ever felt stuck, or as Bob puts it, "You can't move"? Why or why not?
- What do you think the difference is between agreeing with what Jesus says and "doing love"?

HEARING THE WORD

Read Matthew 1:18–23 aloud in the group. Then briefly answer the questions that follow.

[18]This is how the birth of Jesus the Messiah came about: His mother Mary was pledged to be married to Joseph, but before they came together, she was found to be pregnant through the Holy Spirit. [19]Because Joseph her husband was faithful to the law, and yet did not want to expose her to public disgrace, he had in mind to divorce her quietly.

[20]But after he had considered this, an angel of the Lord appeared to him in a dream and said, "Joseph son of David, do not be afraid to take Mary home as your wife, because what is conceived in her is from the Holy Spirit. [21]She will give birth to a son, and you are to give him the name Jesus, because he will save his people from their sins."

[22]All this took place to fulfill what the Lord had said through the prophet: [23]"The virgin will conceive and give birth to a son, and they will call him Immanuel" (which means "God with us").

Do you think it is good news to learn that "God is with us"? Why or why not?

This famous passage about Immanuel is heard often at Christmastime. As a group, can you remember other places in the Bible that God was "with us"? If so, what are they?

WATCH THE VIDEO

Watch the Session 1 video clip, using the space below to take notes. When the video ends, take a moment to reflect on one or two things that you learned, disagreed with, or were surprised by.

GROUP DISCUSSION
First Impressions

1. Before everyone shares in the large group, turn to one or two people next to you and finish this sentence, "After watching the video, one question I now have is ..."

Community Reflection

2. Has someone ever said to you, "I'm with you"? Who was it and what was the occasion? How did it affect you? Have you ever said the same words to someone else? What was that like?

3. Bob says that he quits something every Thursday, and that quitting can be a good thing if you "quit the right stuff." Have you ever quit anything? Was the experience positive or negative? What did it make room for in your life?

4. How do you know the right stuff and the wrong stuff to quit?

5. What does it mean that "God will never quit us"? Does that sound like good news or bad news to you?

6. Have you ever had a dream die? Did it die "alone," as Bob says, or were you with anyone? Did being with someone help?

7. Bob makes a distinction between being in a Bible study with someone and just "being" with someone. What's the difference? Is this a helpful distinction? Why or why not?

8. What did you think of Bob's story about his Young Life leader, Randy? Who has God brought into your life that you can be "a Randy" or "Immanuel" to? To whom do you need to say, "I'm with you"?

PUTTING LOVE INTO ACTION

After Bob tells his story about Randy, he challenges viewers to reach out to someone who has been a "Randy" in their lives and tell that person thank you. That is what we are going to do right now.

Think about your life and consider: Is there a person who has been there with you when the going got rough? Or a person who poured out his or her life to mentor or counsel you? Or someone who talked you out of making a bad choice or talked you into making a good one?

Identify such a person ... and then, right now, reach out to say thanks. Send a text or an email (try Facebook, if you've lost touch). Borrow a smartphone if you didn't bring one or use a piece of paper to write a letter to send later. The more immediate, the better. Just say, "Thank you for being there for me." Be as specific as you feel comfortable, but practice the risk of gratitude.

Reflect together afterward:

- What was this experience like?

- Did anyone get a response from the person he or she contacted? If so, what was it?

- How has this activity been an example of love "doing" things?

CLOSING PRAYER

Close the meeting by praying silently for the person on your left. Pray that each of you will have the courage to "do" the love of Jesus this week, wherever God takes you.

SESSION 1: WHAT LOVE DOES THIS WEEK

You are invited to further explore the challenge of *Love Does* by engaging in any or all of the following activities between sessions. Remember, this part of *Love Does* is not about following rules or doing your homework. These activities (categorized as *Do*, *Reflect*, and *Read*) are designed to give you opportunity to jump into the risk of God's kingdom with both feet. ***Please answer the reflection questions after the activity as a way to: (1) process the experience, and (2) be able to recall it during check-in time at the next session.***

DO: BE A QUITTER

In the video Bob tells a compelling story about the time he quit high school and made a plan to move to Yosemite National Park to rock climb. Even though that plan did not work out very well, it led to an interesting discipline. Once a week Bob quits something.

You are invited to do the same this week. Pick something you need to give up (i.e., texting while you drive) or something you enjoy but decide to put aside for a certain amount of time (i.e., breakfast and lunch for one day, television during the evening, checking email/Facebook after dinner).

Bob's point is that when we quit "stuff," it makes space for Jesus to bring "new stuff" into our lives. Don't rush to fill any new time or emotional space you have with replacement noise, activity, or entertainment. Pay attention in prayer to what Jesus brings into your life so you can say yes to it.

Reflection Questions:

- What did you quit?

- Why did you quit what you did and what was your experience like?

- Did you find anything new came into your life through this process?

- What did you learn about yourself by "being a quitter"? What did you learn about God?

REFLECT: BE SALTY

For the *Reflect* sections of this study guide, we will be going through portions of Jesus' epic teaching in Matthew 5–7, also known as the Sermon on the Mount. In this kingdom-of-God manifesto, Jesus gets extremely practical about what it means to live in God's world God's way and to bring about truth, beauty, and justice as we go.

This week, read Matthew 5:13–16:

> [13]"You are the salt of the earth. But if the salt loses its saltiness, how can it be made salty again? It is no longer good for anything, except to be thrown out and trampled underfoot.
>
> [14]"You are the light of the world. A town built on a hill cannot be hidden. [15]Neither do people light a lamp and put it under a bowl. Instead they put it on its stand, and it gives light to everyone in the house. [16]In the same way, let your light shine before others, that they may see your good deeds and glorify your Father in heaven."

Jesus tells His hearers that they are the salt of the earth and the light of the world. You may be familiar with some of the background in these two metaphors. More than it was known as a flavoring, salt was primarily used to dry and preserve meats in the ancient Near East. Jesus' followers will act in ways that preserve and sustain the earth because God's mission is one of healing and restoration—and that healing and restoration includes the creation itself. If the people of God aren't working to sustain that agenda, they are not doing much good and might as well be tossed out.

Furthermore, Jesus claims that His people are the light of the world. He draws on the common image of a lamp to describe the way that, like light shining into a dark corner, God's people are supposed to reveal things as they really are. Christians believe that God's kingdom is here now, and that things can be here on earth as they are in heaven. This is something we don't simply assert with our lips but actually demonstrate with our lives.

What is so compelling about both of Jesus' metaphors here is how *functional* they are. Jesus seems to expect that the faith of His followers will manifest itself in lives of action that are useful to and positive for the here and now.

Reflection Questions:

- What else do you think Jesus meant when He talked about being salt and light?

- What are the good ways you have seen Christians be "salty" with their lives and faith? Are there negative ways you have seen Christians be "salty" with their faith?

- Is it possible to snuff out your light with the way you try to be salt?

- Where are you being "salty" in your Christianity? Where do you want to grow?

READ: "JUST SAY YES"

Read Chapter 9, "Just Say Yes," in the *Love Does* book.

Reflection Questions:

- Did you have a positive or negative reaction to Bob's story?

- In this chapter Bob says, "I think God sometimes uses the completely inexplicable events in our lives to point us toward Him" (p. 64). Do you think this is true? Why or why not? Have you ever had an "inexplicable event" point you toward God? What inexplicable events are happening in your life right now?

- Is it hard or easy for you to say yes? Why did you answer as you did? How has saying or not saying yes affected your faith for the last year?

SESSION 2

....

FREE TO FAIL

We are no longer defined by our failures.
We are defined by Christ.
Loves Does *video*

INTRODUCTION

Most people, if they are honest, hate to fail. However, if you asked them why they hate failing, you might not get a great answer. They may say, "Because failing stinks." Agreed. It does. That's obvious. But *why* does it stink? *Why* do we hate to fail?

The reason we hate to fail is the same reason we hate finding awkward pictures of ourselves in old photo albums. It's embarrassing! Failure shakes up the fantasy that we're in control of things and makes us feel vulnerable.

Vulnerability. Now we're getting somewhere.

Feeling vulnerable *is* a scary thing. It's not a place many people want to be. However, it is exactly the place that God so often meets us and changes our lives. Think about it: if everything we did succeeded, we might never learn to trust God at all. And if we're not trusting God, we'll start trusting something else, and then we'll lose our way pretty quickly. However, once we've failed—even just once—and experienced God's love and acceptance in that place of exposure and vulnerability, things start changing.

This week in *Love Does* we'll explore the nature of failure, how it works, and what God does with it. How have you dealt with failure in the past? Do you handle it well now? Where has God been in your failure? Hang on to these questions as we jump into Session 2, because maybe your failures are actually opportunities. Opportunities to ask not "Who am I now that I've failed?" but "Who is God leading me to become?"

CHECKING IN

As you begin, go around the group and answer this question:

What was your first job, and do you have good memories or bad memories of the experience?

Last week you were invited to act in the "What Love Does This Week" section of the study.

- Did you do at least one of the activities? If so, which one(s)? If not, why not?
- What are some of the things you wrote down in reflection?
- Did you learn anything about yourself by engaging in these experiments?
- Did you learn anything about God?

HEARING THE WORD

Read John 21:15–19 aloud in the group. Then briefly answer the questions that follow.

[15]When they had finished eating, Jesus said to Simon Peter, "Simon son of John, do you love me more than these?"

"Yes, Lord," he said, "you know that I love you."

Jesus said, "Feed my lambs."

[16]Again Jesus said, "Simon son of John, do you love me?"

He answered, "Yes, Lord, you know that I love you."

Jesus said, "Take care of my sheep."

[17]The third time he said to him, "Simon son of John, do you love me?"

Peter was hurt because Jesus asked him the third time, "Do you love me?" He said, "Lord, you know all things; you know that I love you."

Jesus said, "Feed my sheep. [18]Very truly I tell you, when you were younger you dressed yourself and went where you wanted; but when you are old you will stretch out your hands, and someone else will dress you and lead you where you do not want to go." [19]Jesus said this to indicate the kind of death by which Peter would glorify God. Then he said to him, "Follow me!"

What has Jesus' and Peter's history been before this story? Why do you think Jesus asks Peter the same question three different times?

What does it say about God that Jesus takes Peter back as a disciple? What does it say about Peter that he accepts this reinstatement?

If you were Peter, how would you have responded to Jesus' questions?

WATCH THE VIDEO

Watch the Session 2 video clip, using the space below to take notes. When the video ends, take a moment to reflect on one or two things that you learned, disagreed with, or were surprised by.

GROUP DISCUSSION
First Impressions

1. Before everyone shares in the large group, turn to one or two people next to you and finish this sentence, "After watching the video, one question I now have is ..."

Community Reflection

2. Have you ever utterly failed? What happened?

3. Does God lead us into failures? Bob says yes. What do you think and why?

4. Bob says, "We are no longer defined by our failures. We are defined by Christ." What does this mean, and do you think it's true? Have you ever experienced it?

5. In the video Bob says, "Because most of us are afraid of failing, we end up faking it and acting like somebody who isn't us." Have you ever play-acted to be someone you're not? Who or what did you pretend to be?

6. When you are tempted to fake it, think about whom you are tempted to act like. What does that image say about what you're afraid of? What does it say about who you are afraid to become?

7. Bob tells a story about posing in a wax museum and suggests that he is a poser when he tries to live into someone else's calling instead of his own. Do you know what your calling is? What are you doing to be faithful to that calling? (If you don't know your calling, brainstorm with the group to determine one step you can take toward discovering it.)

PUTTING LOVE INTO ACTION

In the video Bob mentions that Jesus gave people, such as Peter, nicknames. These nicknames were not based on who the person used to be but on who the person was becoming. Read Matthew 16:17–19:

> [17]Jesus replied, "Blessed are you, Simon son of Jonah, for this was not revealed to you by flesh and blood, but by my Father in heaven. [18]And I tell you that you are Peter, and on this rock I will build my church, and the gates of Hades will not overcome it. [19]I will give you the keys of the kingdom of heaven; whatever you bind on earth will be bound in heaven, and whatever you loose on earth will be loosed in heaven."

In the space provided below, jot down one of your most "epic" fails. It should be a failure that is hard to shake, one that follows you around and causes regret. Be honest, because no one will read this unless you choose to share it.

Next, get two sticker nametags from your group leader. On one of the nametags write down a nickname you have given to yourself because of this failure. Again, be as honest as you are comfortable.

Now, take a deep breath and write down a nickname that you think Jesus would give you based on who you are becoming. Briefly consider: How are the nicknames different? How are they related? How can you tell when a nickname comes from God and when it comes from elsewhere?

When everyone has finished, take turns in the group sharing your old nickname. Then, like Bob with his tickets, tear up the nametag and throw it away. Be as dramatic or subtle as you want. Once you've thrown away your old nickname, share your new nickname and stick that nametag on your shirt.

Afterward reflect together:

• Was this activity hard or easy? Why?

- What makes for a good "Jesus nickname"? How is it different from the old nickname you were given?

- How is this exercise an example of love "doing"?

CLOSING PRAYER

Close the session by praying together the words Jesus taught His disciples to pray in the Sermon on the Mount:

Our Father in heaven,
hallowed be your name,
your kingdom come,
your will be done,
    on earth as it is in heaven.
Give us today our daily bread.
And forgive us our debts
    as we also have forgiven our debtors.
And lead us not into temptation,
    but deliver us from the evil one.

Matthew 6:9–13

SESSION 2: WHAT LOVE DOES THIS WEEK

DO: FAIL . . . ON PURPOSE

Bob talks about how our failures become opportunities for God to break pieces off of us so there's more for Him to work with. This week you're going to give God some new raw material.

One of the deep, inner dynamics of experiencing the love of God is recognizing when you are in a place of failure and receiving love right then and there. This is hard to do. When we fail, we want to judge (ourselves or others), get angry, or make excuses to protect our hearts. We end up only doing things we already know we'll be good at so we don't have to experience struggle. What if, instead, we *intentionally* put ourselves in a place of failure and then practice keeping our heart open toward God and receiving His love? Here's how this works:

Think of an activity you know you're not very good at or is a challenge for you. Some suggestions are listed here, or you can pick your own:

- ❏ Take a class at the gym or engage in an exercise that you don't normally do.
- ❏ Write a poem and read it aloud to another person.
- ❏ Dance where others can see you.
- ❏ Write a five-minute speech on something that matters to you. Get at least two or three people together (maybe even members of your *Love Does* study) and present the speech.
- ❏ Other: _____.

Don't choose an activity that could have serious consequences or is foolish (running a marathon with no training or not finishing a project at work).

Once you determine your activity, pick a time this week, say a prayer, and do it. It will likely be frustrating, difficult, and possibly embarrassing. However, try to stay open to God's love, remember your new "Jesus nickname," and see what happens.

Reflection Questions:

- What was the experience like?

- What was your initial impulse when the going got tough?

- Was it easy or difficult to receive the love of God in the midst of failure?

- How might this lesson be transferrable to other areas of your life?

REFLECT: MAKE IT RIGHT

Continuing in Jesus' Sermon on the Mount, read Matthew 5:21–26:

> [21]"You have heard that it was said to the people long ago, 'You shall not murder, and anyone who murders will be subject to judgment.' [22]But I tell you that anyone who is angry with a brother or sister will be subject to judgment. Again, anyone who says to a brother or sister, 'Raca,' is answerable to the court. And anyone who says, 'You fool!' will be in danger of the fire of hell.
>
> [23]"Therefore, if you are offering your gift at the altar and there remember that your brother or sister has something against you, [24]leave your gift there in front of the altar. First go and be reconciled to them; then come and offer your gift.
>
> [25]"Settle matters quickly with your adversary who is taking you to court. Do it while you are still together on the way, or your adversary may hand you over to the judge, and the judge may hand you over to the officer, and you may be thrown into prison. [26]Truly I tell you, you will not get out until you have paid the last penny."

If you've been around Christianity for a while, you have likely encountered this teaching before. Jesus here expands the boundaries of what it means to love your neighbor as yourself. In the kingdom of God it is not sufficient to simply "not kill someone," because God's agenda is much bigger. God wants to heal the root causes of murder: anger, bitterness, the unforgiving human heart—the dark emotions that gain emotional traction when we tear each other down. This is why Jesus links murder and slander. He is not content to leave us with a gospel of abstinence. Jesus' gospel is a gospel of action.

As the teaching progresses, Jesus exhorts His listeners to go and reconcile with "your brother or sister [who] has something against you" (vv. 23–24). Because God's kingdom is about *active* goodness and not just *inactive* badness, it means that healing the human heart will take work—our work as well as His. People who live out Jesus' way will not just avoid slander but also be proactive in making broken relationships whole again.

Reflection Questions

- Pray about your own relationships this week. Is God showing you a broken one that needs to be made whole? Which one?

- What is your "next right step" in working with God to heal this relationship? For example, can being the one to say "I'm sorry" first get the ball rolling?

- Finish this sentence: The thing that scares me most about this exercise is …

READ: "WEDDING CAKE"

Read Chapter 8, "Wedding Cake," in the *Love Does* book.

Reflection Questions:

- Have you ever had an experience where God used your failures for something good?

- What is the difference between "believing the right stuff" and "doing the right stuff?"

- Bob says Jesus can use us "not when we're broken, but because we're broken." And he notes that the only people Jesus couldn't use were the people who were too "full of themselves or believed the lie that they were who they used to be before they met Him" (p. 57). Do you think Bob is right? Why does Jesus choose to use broken people?

- What does it look like to trust Jesus with your brokenness?

AUDACIOUS LOVE

*Are we missing that the God of the
universe is nuts about us?*

Loves Does *video*

INTRODUCTION

If you've ever tried to use a snorkel, you know how tricky it can be. You have to figure out how to keep it upright and learn to swim so that the top doesn't dip below the water line. However, if you do get water in your snorkel (which always happens), you get to do the coolest thing. You get to spit it out! That's right—you just shoot water right out the top of your snorkel! It's kind of fun, but it also has a purpose. You have to clear all that water *out* before you can take your next breath of air *in* . . . because a snorkel is just a tube and the air you breathe in flows through the same pathway as the air your breathe out. If the top of the snorkel is blocked by water, not only can you not breathe out, you also cannot breathe in.

The same thing is true with love.

The love we have flows from our hearts. Well, not our actual hearts, but from the place that is the center of our being and person. However, our hearts, like the snorkel, are two-way streets. Love flows in and out of our hearts through the same "tube." This is one of the reasons Jesus teaches that there's a connection between loving God and loving our neighbors. If we are open to loving others, then our hearts are open to being loved by God. And if our hearts are open to being loved by God, then they are free to let love flow to our neighbors.

But this is not an easy state to maintain. As we get hurt, betrayed, or rejected throughout the course of our lives, our temptation is to close off our hearts to love. We imagine that if we don't give anyone access to our hearts, we can live free from pain. The problem is, of course, the "snorkel." When we close off the possibility of loving others, we close off our capacity to be loved by God. This is why many of us wither away in life and faith. Our pain and desire for self-protection cause us to cut ourselves off from the source of true life.

This week in *Love Does* we are asked to risk opening parts of our "snorkels" that we may have closed off to the extravagant love of God. Do you think it is easier for you to give love or receive love? Why is that true, and what will it take for you to open yourself to God's love in a new way this week?

CHECKING IN

As you begin, go around the group and answer this question:

What's the biggest favor anyone has ever asked of you?

Last week you were invited to act in the "What Love Does This Week" section of the study.

- Did you do at least one of the activities? If so, which one(s)? If not, why not?
- What are some of the things you wrote down in reflection?
- Did you learn anything about yourself or about God by engaging in these experiments?

HEARING THE WORD

Read 1 John 4:7–12 aloud in the group twice. While the passage is being read, prepare to answer this question: *What does this Scripture say about the relationship between God's love and ours?* After the readings, have two or three participants share their responses, and then answer the additional questions that follow.

> [7]Dear friends, let us love one another, for love comes from God. Everyone who loves has been born of God and knows God. [8]Whoever does not love does not know God, because God is love. [9]This is how God showed his love among us: He sent his one and

only Son into the world that we might live through him. [10]This is love: not that we loved God, but that he loved us and sent his Son as an atoning sacrifice for our sins. [11]Dear friends, since God so loved us, we also ought to love one another. [12]No one has ever seen God; but if we love one another, God lives in us and his love is made complete in us.

What does verse 12 mean when it says that God's love is "made complete in us?"

How does our love for one another make God "visible"?

WATCH THE VIDEO

Watch the Session 3 video clip, using the space below to take notes. When the video ends, take a moment to reflect on one or two things that you learned, disagreed with, or were surprised by.

GROUP DISCUSSION
First Impressions

1. Before everyone shares in the large group, turn to one or two people next to you and finish this sentence, "After watching the video, one question I now have is . . ."

Community Reflection

2. How did you like Bob's story about Ryan? Did it make you feel more inspired ("I could do that too!") or condemned ("I've never done anything that creative!")? Why?

3. What can we learn about God's love from the kind of love Ryan demonstrated? Is that kind of love easy or hard to accept?

4. Bob suggests that there's a difference between trying to "win someone over" versus simply "telling them how you feel." Is he right? If not, why not? If so, how do you explain the difference?

5. How do you think this difference might relate to Christian practices such as evangelism?

6. Remember the passage from 1 John we read about God's love? Have you ever experienced God's love through the way someone else treated you? If so, describe the situation. If not, what do you think that kind of love might look like?

7. Has there ever been a circumstance in your life that God used to show you He loved you? What was it and how could you tell it was God who orchestrated it?

PUTTING LOVE INTO ACTION

Bob concludes the video this week by asking if we are missing the fact that the God of the universe is crazy about us. This exercise is designed to help us develop eyes to see the activity, presence, and love of God everywhere.

Read together the story of Jacob and his dream as told in Genesis 28:10 – 17:

^{10}Jacob left Beersheba and set out for Harran. ^{11}When he reached a certain place, he stopped for the night because the sun had set. Taking one of the stones there, he put it under his head and lay down to sleep. ^{12}He had a dream in which he saw a stairway resting on the earth, with its top reaching to heaven, and the angels of God were ascending and descending on it. ^{13}There above it stood the LORD, and he said: "I am the LORD, the God of your father Abraham and the God of Isaac. I will give you and your descendants the land on which you are lying. ^{14}Your descendants will be like the dust of the earth, and you will spread out to the west and to the east, to the north and to the south. All peoples on earth will be blessed through you and your offspring. ^{15}I am with you and will watch over you wherever you go, and I will bring you back to this land. I will not leave you until I have done what I have promised you."

^{16}When Jacob awoke from his sleep, he thought, "Surely the LORD is in this place, and I was not aware of it." ^{17}He was afraid and said, "How awesome is this place! This is none other than the house of God; this is the gate of heaven."

One of the revolutionary things about this story is that Jacob encounters God at a place where no one of that time would ever expect. Jacob was not in a temple or on top of a mountain or at the edge of the sea when he dreamed of heaven and earth meeting. He was nowhere special—literally by the side of the road, a random location.

As a group, watch two or three of today's top-rated videos on YouTube. Nothing is more random that YouTube. The videos will probably range from pop music pieces to kittens playing with socks. Because your group leader will have already checked the appropriateness of each video, all you have to do is relax and ask this question: "God, where is your kingdom already on display in this video?"

Resist the urge to judge the video's content, morality, or even its technique. This exercise is about developing the skill of locating God's presence in unlikely places.

Afterward reflect together:

• What was this experience like for you?

• Where did you see God in these videos?

• Was it hard or easy to find God there?

• How can developing this skill with videos help us see God's love more in our everyday lives?

CLOSING PRAYER

Close by everyone to offering a one-word prayer (yes, just one word!) regarding how you want to experience the love of God.

SESSION 3: WHAT LOVE DOES THIS WEEK

DO: GOD WAS IN THIS PLACE AND I DID NOT KNOW IT, PART 2

Reread the story of Jacob from Genesis 28:10–17:

> [10]Jacob left Beersheba and set out for Harran. [11]When he reached a certain place, he stopped for the night because the sun had set. Taking one of the stones there, he put it under his head and lay down to sleep. [12]He had a dream in which he saw a stairway resting on the earth, with its top reaching to heaven, and the angels of God were ascending and descending on it. [13]There above it stood the LORD, and he said: "I am the LORD, the God of your father Abraham and the God of Isaac. I will give you and your descendants the land on which you are lying. [14]Your descendants will be like the dust of the earth, and you will spread out to the west and to the east, to the north and to the south. All peoples on earth will be blessed through you and your offspring. [15]I am with you and will watch over you wherever you go, and I will bring you back to this land. I will not leave you until I have done what I have promised you."
>
> [16]When Jacob awoke from his sleep, he thought, "Surely the LORD is in this place, and I was not aware of it." [17]He was afraid and said, "How awesome is this place! This is none other than the house of God; this is the gate of heaven."

Your invitation this week is to seek the presence of God in a place "by the side of the road." This could be either a place you go often and don't think to look for God (the grocery story, your daughter's dance class, a work staff meeting, the drop-off line at school, etc.) or a place you wonder if God might not be at all (an abortion clinic, the mall, your town's red-light district).

Go to the place you've selected and then walk through and/or around the area, praying this prayer: "God, show me where Your kingdom and love are already on display in this place and with these people."* As you go, take care to look everyone you pass in the eye and be friendly. If the temptation to judge creeps up, pray, "God, help me to think Your thoughts and feel Your feelings for this place and these people."*

Reflection Questions:

- Where did you find God during this activity?

- Were you surprised?

- What did you learn about love through the process?

READ: "HEARING AID"

Read Chapter 21, "Hearing Aid," in the *Love Does* book.

Reflection Questions:

- Have you ever "heard" God speak to or direct you? How did that work?

---

*Thanks to Mark Scandrette and Re:imagine for these prayers.

- Bob says, "Humans are limited [but] God isn't limited at all. He can communicate to us in any way He wants to anytime He wants to" (p. 140). How, then, are we supposed to listen? What makes listening to God hard for you?

- Bob says that because he doesn't hear from God audibly, he just looks for where Jesus has been. Where have you seen that Jesus has been this week?

- Where has Jesus been in your life the past ten years? "Who" or "what" were some of the messages that He communicated to you?

....

BE NOT AFRAID

Jesus said, "Go live a really, really full life.
One that is chocked full of adventures."
Loves Does *video*

INTRODUCTION

In 1975, the movie *Jaws* broke box office records and was hailed as the one of the summer's blockbusters. However, as celebrated as the movie is for its domestic gross earnings, great performances, and iconic score, *Jaws* is famous for another reason as well. The film's antagonist, a motorized replica of a great white shark, kept breaking down during production. Because of this, the film's director, Steven Spielberg, had to shoot "around" the shark, implying its presence in scenes while never showing it directly to the audience. But instead of making the movie worse, it actually made it better. Not being able to see what the heroes were hunting built such suspense and dread that once the shark was finally "on screen"—out in the light—it was actually a relief. Once you could see it, it was not nearly as intimidating.

The same is true of the things that scare us today.

Our fears have power over us only when they are kept in the dark. Their hiddenness fuels all sorts of shame and humiliation in our lives and drives us to make bad decisions because we are afraid. However, when we name our fears and speak them aloud—especially to someone else—the God of the universe can dispel them with the light of His love. Just like the shark in *Jaws*, our fears become less scary once they are out in the open.

This is a bit of what we're doing in Session 4 of *Love Does*.

What are you afraid of? Are there fears that keep you locked up inside? Is there an anxiety that keeps you from acting and chasing after what Jesus is calling you to? Do you think that addressing these fears head on, exposing them, and maybe even laughing about them will give God a context to bring freedom into your life?

There's a reason God frequently says, "Don't be afraid" in the Scriptures. It's because we don't have to be. Fear, in many respects, is a choice … and when we lean on our Creator and entrust ourselves to His love, we find that the things we fear most are not so scary after all.

CHECKING IN

As you begin, go around the group and answer this question:

What is one thing you were scared of as a child that you're not scared of today?

Last week you were invited to act in the "What Love Does This Week" section of the study.

- Did you do at least one of the activities? If so, which one(s)? If not, why not?
- Did you find God in any unexpected places? If so, which ones?
- Did you learn anything about yourself or about God by engaging in these experiments?

HEARING THE WORD

Read Mark 6:45–52 aloud in the group. Then briefly answer the questions that follow.

[45]Immediately Jesus made his disciples get into the boat and go on ahead of him to Bethsaida, while he dismissed the crowd. [46]After leaving them, he went up on a mountainside to pray.

[47]Later that night, the boat was in the middle of the lake, and he was alone on land. [48]He saw the disciples straining at the oars, because the wind was against them. Shortly before dawn he went out to them, walking on the lake. He was about to pass by them, [49]but when they saw him walking on the lake, they thought he was a ghost. They cried out, [50]because they all saw him and were terrified.

Immediately he spoke to them and said, "Take courage! It is I. Don't be afraid." [51]Then he climbed into the boat with them, and the wind died down. They were completely amazed, [52]for they had not understood about the loaves; their hearts were hardened.

What does this story mean to you?

Why does God's activity sometimes make us afraid?

WATCH THE VIDEO

Watch the Session 4 video clip, using the space below to take notes. When the video ends, take a moment to reflect on one or two things that you learned, disagreed with, or were surprised by.

GROUP DISCUSSION
First Impressions

1. Before everyone shares in the large group, turn to one or two people next to you and finish this sentence, "After watching the video one question I now have is ..."

Community Reflection

2. Bob uses the phrase "live a full life." What do you think makes a life "full"?

3. Bob shares how Adam saw the potential in the boat for adventure. He saw that same potential in his life. How do you see your life? Is there a potential for adventure? Why or why not?

4. What things draw you away from magnetic North, away from the life God wants you to have?

5. What's the difference between being brave and being foolish when it comes to stepping out to trust God?

6. Bob says that by using Scripture on one corner and people who know God and are wise on another, we can triangulate where we are in life. Does this work? If so, how?

7. If your life is a boat, describe where it is in relationship to the dock. Is it tied tightly? Is it free to sail? Share where you are today and then what helps or hinders you from untying the boat.

PUTTING LOVE INTO ACTION

Now that we have discussed the power of spontaneously stepping into adventure with God, we are going to practice this posture with a classic group game: the human knot.

Divide participants into small groups of six to eight people. Have each group stand in a tight circle and place their hands into the center. Grab the hand of someone across from you in the circle (if possible, do not grab the hand of the person immediately next to you). Once everyone is holding two other hands, the group has ten minutes to "untie" the knot without letting go of each other. When you are done, the group should be in a circle.

Your temptation might be to grumble or sit this one out. Please don't. Practice seeing the *Love Does* possibility for adventure in this activity rather than refusing to do something you don't like.

When your knot is untied, or after ten minutes are up, reflect together:

- What was it like for you to have to just "jump into" the game?

- On a scale of fun to annoying, where did this activity land for you?

- How does practicing adventure work against fear in our lives?

CLOSING PRAYER

Close the session by reciting together this Collect from the Book of Common Prayer:

> O God our King, by the resurrection of your Son Jesus Christ on the first day of the week, you conquered sin, put death to flight, and gave us the hope of everlasting life: Redeem all our days by this victory; forgive our sins, banish our fears, make us bold to praise you and to do your will; and steel us to wait for the consummation of your kingdom on the last great Day; through the same Jesus Christ our Lord. Amen.

SESSION 4: WHAT LOVE DOES THIS WEEK

DO: WELCOME A STRANGER

Read Hebrews 13:1–3:

> [1]Keep on loving one another as brothers and sisters. [2]Do not forget to show hospitality to strangers, for by so doing some people have shown hospitality to angels without knowing it. [3]Continue to remember those in prison as if you were together with them in prison, and those who are mistreated as if you yourselves were suffering.

Behind some of our most primal fears is often a basic fear of the unknown. The unfamiliar or unseen is usually scariest to us. This is why one of the classic Christian disciplines that can heal our fear is the practice of hospitality. Through hospitality—welcoming strangers (or the unknown) into our home, reaching out to the sick and needy—we turn our fear into friendship and do another small part in bringing heaven to earth.

This week you are invited to welcome a stranger in one of three ways:

First, you can have a meal with a "stranger." This can be anything from buying lunch for and eating with a panhandler to inviting some new neighbors over for dinner. Ask God to show you which stranger to welcome. The second option is to visit someone who is sick, and the third is to go to someone in need. Is there someone in the hospital or a shut-in you could call on? Is there someone in prison you could visit or write a letter to? Again, ask God to show you someone already in your life orbit to whom you might extend hospitality.

Choose one of these three ideas and then act!

Reflection Questions:

- What did you learn about yourself and about God through this exercise?

- Would living this way more often make you less afraid? Why or why not?

REFLECT: GO DOWN TO THE WATER

Continuing in Jesus' Sermon on the Mount, read Matthew 6:25–34:

> [25]"Therefore I tell you, do not worry about your life, what you will eat or drink; or about your body, what you will wear. Is not life more than food, and the body more than clothes? [26]Look at the birds of the air; they do not sow or reap or store away in barns, and yet your heavenly Father feeds them. Are you not much more valuable than they? [27]Can any one of you by worrying add a single hour to your life?
>
> [28]"And why do you worry about clothes? See how the flowers of the field grow. They do not labor or spin. [29]Yet I tell you that not even Solomon in all his splendor was dressed like one of these. [30]If that is how God clothes the grass of the field, which is here today and tomorrow is thrown into the fire, will he not much more clothe you—you of little faith? [31]So do not worry, saying, 'What shall we eat?' or 'What shall we drink?' or 'What

shall we wear?' ³²For the pagans run after all these things, and your heavenly Father knows that you need them. ³³But seek first his kingdom and his righteousness, and all these things will be given to you as well. ³⁴Therefore do not worry about tomorrow, for tomorrow will worry about itself. Each day has enough trouble of its own."

Jesus moves toward the conclusion of this grand teaching in Matthew's gospel with a command not to worry. Taken out of context, it can feel like an unachievable demand. *Don't worry? Are you crazy, Jesus? I have no control over that, and now I'm worried I can't live up to your expectation not to worry!*

Relax. This is not what Jesus is getting at.

There is a flow to the Sermon on the Mount. It's going somewhere. And where Jesus is taking the crowds when He tells them not to worry is at the conclusion of a long section about entrusting ourselves to God. God is trustworthy, Jesus explains, and the more we accept that truth and practice it, the freer we become from worry and anxiety.

Bob began this *Love Does* session by talking about how he likes to be "down by the water," because for him it is there that life slows down and its relentless cadence is disrupted. So, your invitation is to take this meditation and find some water to sit beside. It can be the ocean, a lake, a river, a swimming pool, or a decorative fountain. Wherever you go, let the water symbolize the place where life slows down for a bit.

Once you arrive at your destination, take a few deep breaths and practice just being with God. You can reflect on where your life is with God and where He wants to take you next. Or you might consider your fears, where they might come from, and what it will take to surrender them to God. Whatever you do, don't fill this time by the water with activity. Too much activity (even if it's good stuff like reading the Bible) can actually rob us of the benefits of resting. Take the time to just *be*.

Once you've returned from the water's edge, reflect on the experience.

Reflection Questions:

- Where did you choose to go and how long did you stay?

- Describe the experience with one word.

- Did anything distract you while you were alone? Does that tell you anything about yourself?

- How could a practice like this be part of your everyday life with God?

FOLLOW ME

*Jesus says let's go and do stuff and we'll find out
who I am and who you are along the way.*
Loves Does *video*

INTRODUCTION

Once upon a time there were two pilgrims going on a road trip with some friends. Pilgrim A was the kind of person who wanted to have every gas-, food-, and potty-stop mapped out ahead of time. When selecting routes, Pilgrim A always picked the most direct one (so that they would arrive at their destination on schedule), and any sightseeing needed to be planned in advance (nothing spontaneous).

Pilgrim B, however, was happy to just go with the flow. It didn't matter to her when and where the group stopped, ate, or arrived, nor did she care what route they took. And if some interesting attraction came up along the way, Pilgrim B would gladly detour the whole caravan to see it.

When Jesus invites us to follow Him, He doesn't tell us every step of the journey ahead. There are adventures and discoveries awaiting us that we could never anticipate. However, that doesn't mean Jesus' disciples should never make a plan. In fact, when we read the Gospels, it seems like Jesus is looking for disciples who start with the passion of Pilgrim B and then adopt the practicality of Pilgrim A. He is looking for people with enough enthusiasm to abandon their vocations to follow Him, yet He expects those disciples to mature into women and men who can be intentional about bringing God's kingdom here and now. And as the Gospel stories progress, we start to see why. Jesus' intention isn't to stick around. His plan is to leave and turn everything over to His disciples with the guidance of the Holy Spirit to show them the next steps.

The final session of *Love Does* will explore how to bring our passions and plans together. Do you know folks who have integrated planning into their praying? What did that look like? Furthermore, what, if anything, do you think God might be calling you to make a plan about? Consider all of this as we conclude our *Love Does* journey, and be listening for where the Spirit may be nudging you next.

CHECKING IN

As you begin, go around the group and answer this question:

Which of the world's problems makes you feel the most overwhelmed because it is so big and complicated?

Last week you were invited to act in the "What Love Does This Week" section of the study.

- Did you do at least one of the activities? If so, which one(s)? If not, why not?
- What was your experience like? (Share anything you wrote down in your reflections.)
- What did you learn about yourself through this process? What did you learn about God?

HEARING THE WORD

Read the following Scripture passages aloud in the group. If possible, have a different reader for each passage. Then answer the questions that follow.

Matthew 4:18–20

[18]As Jesus was walking beside the Sea of Galilee, he saw two brothers, Simon called Peter and his brother Andrew. They were casting a net into the lake, for they were fishermen. [19]"Come, follow me," Jesus said, "and I will send you out to fish for people." [20]At once they left their nets and followed him.

Matthew 16:24

Then Jesus said to his disciples, "Whoever wants to be my disciple must deny themselves and take up their cross and follow me.

Luke 18:18–22

[18]A certain ruler asked him, "Good teacher, what must I do to inherit eternal life?"

[19]"Why do you call me good?" Jesus answered. "No one is good—except God alone. [20]You know the commandments: 'You shall not commit adultery, you shall not murder, you shall not steal, you shall not give false testimony, honor your father and mother.'"

[21]"All these I have kept since I was a boy," he said.

[22]When Jesus heard this, he said to him, "You still lack one thing. Sell everything you have and give to the poor, and you will have treasure in heaven. Then come, follow me."

Name two or three things these passages have in common.

In each case, following Jesus means leaving one thing behind for something better. What do you imagine Jesus is asking you to leave behind in order to better follow Him today?

WATCH THE VIDEO

Watch the Session 5 video clip, using the space below to take notes. When the video ends, take a moment to reflect on one or two things that you learned, disagreed with, or were surprised by.

GROUP DISCUSSION
First Impressions

1. Before everyone shares in the large group, turn to one or two people next to you and finish this sentence, "After watching the video, one question I now have is ..."

Community Reflection

2. Bob says that Jesus loves justice. What is justice? What does God's justice look like?

3. In the video, Bob challenges us to consider making a difference for God. A big difference, not a small difference! How does this challenge to dream big affect you? Is it invigorating or intimidating, or a little of both? Explain.

4. Bob asks, "What if we're the ones who aren't efficient with our love?" What do you think he means by this question? Are you too efficient with your love? Not efficient enough?

5. What's the difference between waving at Jesus and following Him? Is there an area of your life where it's easier to wave to Him than to follow? Why do you think that's the case, and what might you do to change?

PUTTING LOVE INTO ACTION

For the past four weeks, after the *Love Does* group discussion, we have engaged in a very practical activity designed to put love into action. Heretofore, these activities have been provided *for* you. This week it's *your* turn.

During check-in, you were invited to share which of the world's problems makes you feel most overwhelmed. Then, during the video, Bob challenged all of us to follow the lead of his friend John and consider what our "Two Bunk" caper might be. Now we are mashing these two ideas together. You get to ask where God's people are hurting in the world and what your next move could be to do something big about it.

For the next 5–10 minutes, use one of the laptop computers, tablets, or smartphones to research the problem you described as overwhelming. Make notes in the space provided below on the size and scope of the problem as well as anything you discover about how to help. Then cook up the biggest, most audacious scheme you can think of to help be part of the solution to this problem.

My Research/My Plan

Now, go around the group and each person share both the problem and the audacious solution. Then, as a group, brainstorm what each individual's "next step" can be. The goal is for every person in the study to leave with at least one concrete action he or she can take to live out a life where "Love Does." And if you have trouble thinking of a "next step," give Bob a call. His number is in the back of the *Love Does* book!

My Next Step

CLOSING REFLECTIONS

Use these sentence fill-ins to help the group reflect on the *Love Does* study experience as a whole.

- Because of my *Love Does* experience, I used to think _____, but now I know _____.
- The best thing about this *Love Does* experience was _____. The worst thing was _____.
- If I could describe my *Love Does* experience in one word, it would be: _____.

CLOSING PRAYER

Close the meeting the same way we closed Session 1: praying silently for the person on your left. Pray for the courage to "do" the love of Jesus as each of you leaves this place and goes fearlessly wherever God leads.

SESSION 5: WHAT LOVE DOES THIS WEEK

DO: PULL OFF YOUR CAPER

The "Do" challenge for this week is to follow up on the "next step" you envisioned with your group during Session 5. This is part of the grand adventure we are invited into when we follow Jesus. Let's not pay our discipleship lip service only. Get out there this week and take that next step.

If you already have taken that next step, send some of your group members an email to let them know how it went. Then, start scheming for where God might be leading you to go next!

REFLECT: HEAR AND DO

Read this concluding section of the Sermon on the Mount from Matthew 7:24–27:

> [24]"Therefore everyone who hears these words of mine and puts them into practice is like a wise man who built his house on the rock. [25]The rain came down, the streams rose, and the winds blew and beat against that house; yet it did not fall, because it had its foundation on the rock. [26]But everyone who hears these words of mine and does not put them into practice is like a foolish man who built his house on sand. [27]The rain came down, the streams rose, and the winds blew and beat against that house, and it fell with a great crash."

As we have explored in this study, Jesus' "kingdom manifesto," the Sermon on the Mount, has a flow. It's not a collection of disconnected proverbs but a train that's headed somewhere. That destination is found in the passage you just read.

Jesus has been inviting His hearers to fully entrust themselves to God and His way of living. The kind of life Jesus describes is how humans were created to live and where they will find life, hope, justice, and peace. However, He warns that this way of life is not always easy.

Sometimes we get the impression (or are explicitly taught) that if we just keep close enough to Jesus on the narrow path, everything will work out okay: we'll be immune from suffering and get a pass on tragedy. Sadly, nothing could be further from the truth. Storms, as Jesus points out, will come. They are unavoidable. They are the stuff of life. Everyone will encounter them. The difference is where you "build your house."

But Jesus says that if we put His teachings into practice (in other words, become His followers), we will be like a house built on the rock. When life's storms batter us, we'll have the inner strength to stand firm against the wind and rain. And when the sun comes out again, we'll still be standing—because we trust the Son. Do you believe it?

Reflection Questions:

- When you consider Jesus' call to follow Him, do you think about the storms?

- Do you think there are any storms that are more than you and God could handle?

- What do you think a "house built on sand" looks like? Why doesn't it hold up in a storm?

READ: "JUST SAY YES"

Read Chapter 30, "Palms Up," in the *Love Does* book.

Reflection Questions

- Do you tend to have a hot or cool temper?

- Bob says, "It was Jesus who taught me there was nothing I could really lose if I had Him" (p. 205). How does this quote resonate with you? Do you find it to be true in your life?

- Think about a situation in your life about which you are tempted to feel defensive or lose your cool. Sit in a chair, put your palms up, and recall that very situation. Use the posture of sitting with your palms up as a prayer: a prayer that God will make you strong enough to not be afraid of being vulnerable, a prayer that you will follow Jesus in keeping your palms up. Write about how this prayer experience impacted you.

ADDITIONAL RESOURCES FOR GROUP LEADERS

Thank you for giving of your time and talent to lead a *Love Does* group study.

The *Love Does* experience is as a five-session study built around weekly small group gatherings (or however often your group meets). As group leader, imagine yourself as the host of a dinner party whose job is to manage all the behind-the-scenes details so your guests can focus on each other and interaction around the topic.

You need not answer all the questions or reteach the content—the book, video, and study guide do most of that work. This makes your small group more of a learning community—a place to process, question, and reflect on what the author, Bob Goff, is teaching.

Make sure everyone in the group gets a copy of this study guide. Encourage them to write in their guide and bring it with them every week. This will keep everyone on the same page and help the session run more smoothly. Likewise, encourage every participant (or every couple) to get a copy of the *Love Does* book so they can complete the suggested readings in the "What Love

Does This Week" sections. If this is not possible, see if anyone from the group is willing to donate an extra copy or two for sharing. Giving everyone access to all the material will position this study to be as rewarding an experience as possible.

HOSPITALITY

As group leader, you'll want to create an environment conducive to sharing and learning. A church sanctuary or classroom may not be ideal for this kind of meeting because those venues can feel formal and less intimate. Wherever you choose, make sure there is enough comfortable seating for everyone and, if possible, arrange the seats in a semicircle so everyone can see the video player easily. This will make transition between the video and group conversation more efficient and natural.

Also, try to get to the meeting site early so you can greet participants as they arrive, especially newcomers. Simple refreshments create a welcoming atmosphere and can be a wonderful addition to a group study gathering. If you do serve food, try to take into account any food allergies or dietary restrictions group members may have. Also, if you meet in a home, find out if the house has pets (in case there are any allergies) and even consider offering child care to couples with children who want to attend. Finally, be sure your media technology is working properly. Managing these details upfront will make the rest of your group experience flow more smoothly and provide a welcoming space in which to engage the content of *Love Does*.

LEADING YOUR GROUP

Once everyone has arrived, it is time to begin the group. If you are new to small group leadership, what follows are some simple tips to making your group time healthy, enjoyable, and effective.

First, consider beginning the meeting with a word of prayer. Then remind people to silence and put away their mobile phones. This is a way to say yes to being present to each other and to God.

Next, invite a volunteer to read the session's introduction from this study guide to focus everyone on the week's topic. Then, after the "Checking In" time (see below), your group will engage in a simple Bible study called "Hearing the Word" drawn from the content of the video. You do not need to be a biblical scholar to lead this effectively. Your role is only to open up conversation by using the instructions provided and invite the group into the text.

Now that the group is fully engaged, it is time to watch the video (the videos range from 10–15 minutes, depending on the session; space is provided in the study guide for jotting notes). The content of each *Love Does* session is inspiring but challenging, so there is built-in time for personal reflection before anyone is asked to respond to the "First Impressions" question. Don't skip over this part. Internal processors will need the more intimate space to sort through their thoughts and questions, and it will make the "Community Reflection" time more fruitful.

Continue with the "Community Reflection" questions. Encourage everyone in the group to participate, but make sure that those who do not want to share know they do not have to (especially as the questions become more personal). As the discussion progresses, follow up with questions like, "Tell me more about that," or "Why did you answer the way you did?" This will allow participants to deepen their reflections and it invites meaningful sharing in a nonthreatening way.

Each session features multiple questions. You do not have to use them all or follow along in chronological order. Pick and choose questions based on either the needs of your group or how the conversation is flowing. Also, don't be afraid of silence. Offering a question and allowing up to thirty seconds of silence gives people space to think about how they want to respond and also gives them time to do so.

As group leader, you are the boundary keeper for your group. Do not let anyone (yourself included) dominate the discussion. Keep an eye out for group members who might be tempted to "attack" folks they disagree with or who try to "fix" those having struggles. Such behaviors can derail a group's momentum. Model active listening and encourage everyone in your group to do the same. This will make your group time a "safe space" and foster the kind of community that God can use to change people.

"Community Reflection" will be followed by the most dynamic part of the weekly group study—"Putting Love into Action"—during which time participants are invited to put what they have learned into practice. **Read the instructions for this section ahead of time as all but one of the activities require special materials.** Reading ahead will allow you to ask group members to bring any items you might need but don't have; it also will give you a sense of how to lead your group through the experience. Use the following supply list to make sure you have everything you need.

Supply List

Session 1:

- ❏ One or more smartphones (and/or a laptop with Internet capability)
- ❏ Paper (for letter writing)
- ❏ Pens

Session 2:

- ❏ A trash can
- ❏ Stick-on name tags (enough for each person in the group to have two)
- ❏ Pens

Session 3:

- ❏ Laptop with Internet connection
- ❏ A browser window containing a prescreened, popular YouTube video
- ❏ Portable speakers (optional—depending on group size)

Session 4:

No special materials are needed for this activity, but just a reminder to the leader that participants are NOT to take hold of the hand of the person standing next to them in the circle.

Also remind the group to keep a "risk-taking, adventurous" attitude for this activity.

(cont.)

Session 5:
❑ One or more laptops, tablets, or smartphones (enough for everyone in the group to do Internet research on their "caper")—email group members before this meeting to remind them to bring their devices
❑ WiFi for all devices
❑ Current newspapers or magazines (for a non-digital exploration)

Lastly, even though closing prayer suggestions are provided, please feel free to strike out on your own. Just make sure you do something intentional to mark the end of the meeting. It may also be helpful to take time before or after the closing prayer to go over that week's "What Love Does" options and encourage everyone to try at least one of the activities.

DEBRIEFING "WHAT LOVE DOES THIS WEEK"

Each week there is inter-session work called "What Love Does This Week." Everyone is invited to choose one or more of these activities to participate in between group meetings. Your job is to help everyone debrief these experiences at the next session's "Checking In."

Debriefing these activities is a bit different than responding to a video because the content comes from the participants' real lives. Though there are specific questions for each debriefing time, the basic experiences that you want the group to reflect on are:

- What was the best thing about the activity?
- What was the hardest thing?
- What did I learn about myself?
- What did I learn about God?

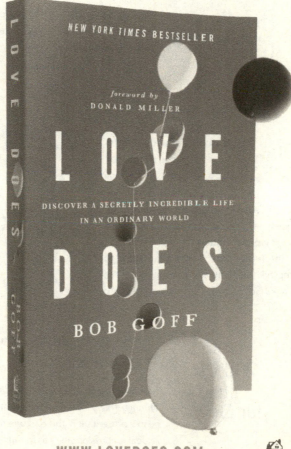

Tools for Your Church or Small Group

You'll Get Through This DVD
978-0-8499-5997-4 | $26.99

Max Lucado leads six video sessions, which will help small group participants apply the truth of Genesis 50:20 to their own lives. What Satan intends for evil, God redeems for good.

You'll Get Through This Study Guide
978-0-8499-5998-1 | $10.99

Filled with Scripture study, discussion questions, and practical ideas designed to lead group members through the story of Joseph and remind us all to trust God to trump evil, this guide is an integral part of the You'll Get Through This small group study.

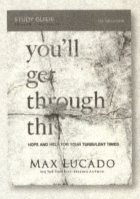

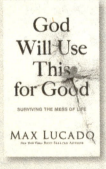

God Will Use This for Good
978-0-8499-4754-4 | $2.99

Featuring key selections from You'll Get Through This, scripture promises, and a gospel presentation, this 64-page booklet is ideal for passing along to friends who are facing turbulent times.

Tools for Your Church or Small Group

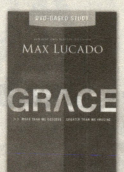

GRACE DVD-Based Study
978-1-4016-7582-0 | $39.99

Join Max Lucado through seven DVD sessions ideal for small-group settings.

GRACE Participant's Guide
978-1-4016-7584-4 | $9.99

Filled with Scripture study, discussion questions, and practical ideas designed to lead group members to a deeper understanding and application of grace, this guide is an integral part of the *GRACE* small-group study.

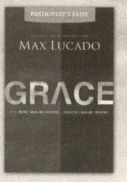

Shaped by Grace
978-0-8499-6450-3 | $2.99

Featuring key selections from *GRACE*, this 64-page booklet is ideal for introducing friends and family to the transforming work of God's grace.

All In Study Guide with DVD

You Are One Decision Away from a Totally Different Life

Mark Batterson

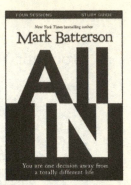

The gospel costs nothing, but it demands everything!

All In, a four-session video-based Bible study by *New York Times* bestselling author Mark Batterson, is a call to complete consecration. If Jesus is not Lord of all, then He is not Lord at all. It's all or nothing.

Many people think they are following Jesus, but the reality is, they've invited Jesus to follow them. They call him Savior, but they've never surrendered to him as Lord. Are you following Jesus? Or have you invited Jesus to follow you?

Over the course of these four sessions you will be challenged to make defining decisions and follow Jesus in ways you may have never dreamed before. If you go **all in**, God will show up and show off His power and glory in your life!

The DVD includes four eighteen-to-twenty-minute video teaching sessions from Mark Batterson. The study guide enhances the experience of the video teaching and includes:

- discussion questions
- video teaching notes
- between-session personal studies
- journal prompts

Available in stores and online!

Fight: A DVD Study

Winning the Battles
That Matter Most

Craig Groeschel

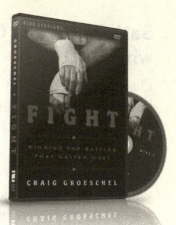

Author and pastor Craig Groeschel
helps you uncover who you really
are — a man created in the image of
God with a warrior's heart — and how
to fight the good fight for what's right.
You will find the strength to fight the
battles you know you need to fight — the ones that determine the
state of your heart, the quality of your marriage, and the spiritual
health of your family. The battles that make you dependent on God
as the source of your strength. The battles that make you come alive.

In this five-session video study (study guide sold separately),
Craig will also look at examples from the Bible, especially someone
with some startling similarities to most men today — our good buddy
Samson. Yep, the dude with the rippling biceps and hippie hair and
a thing for Delilah. You may be surprised how much we have in common with this guy. Things didn't work out so well for him in the end.
But by looking at his life, you'll learn how to defeat the demons that
make strong men weak. You'll become who God made you to be: a
man who knows how to fight for what's right.

You have the heart of a warrior.

Learn how to fight with faith, with prayer, and with the Word of
God. Then, when your enemy begins to attack, fight for the righteous
cause that God gave you. Draw a line in the sand. Make your enemy
pay. Make sure he gets the message. Don't cross a warrior. Don't
mess with this man of God. Come out fighting.

And don't show up for this fight unarmed. Use the weapons God
gave you, and you'll win. Can you feel it? It's inside you.

It's time to fight like a man.

Satisfied Study Guide with DVD

Discovering Contentment in a World of Consumption

Jeff Manion

Why is a contented, satisfied life so eva-sive? What deep hungers drive the reckless purchasing habits, out-of-control accumulation, and crazy consumer lifestyle for so many of us? And why are we often driven more by what our neighbors own than what will truly make us happy?

In this DVD-based Bible study, popular communicator and pastor Jeff Manion provides an inspiring and transformative vision for living a deeply contented life in the midst of our consumer-driven, materialistic, and often shallow culture. In light of our surroundings, Manion asks a critical question: Is it possible to live a deeply satisfied life, one of great inner joy, even as dreams seem to fade?

Satisfied draws richly from seven passages of Scripture, exploring the way in which these messages were received by the original readers and how these passages can alter the way we view wealth, accumulation, and ultimate contentment today.

This study guide contains video notes, individual or group reflection questions, and between-session personal projects enhancing your journey through each of the video sessions.

Available in stores and online!